This book belongs to:

_____

the TWELVE outlaws
BIBLE STUDY FOR TEENS

T.S. Dobson

CAMELLIA
HOUSE PUBLISHING

the TWELVE outlaws
T.S. Dobson

a Bible Study for Teens

Copyright 2014 by Teresa Scott Dobson (author of The Fruit of the Spirit: for Preteens)

ISBN-13: 978-1502380630
ISBN-10: 1502380633

All Scripture quotations in this book are taken from the King James Version, New International Version, and New Living Translation.

Cover art by Teresa Scott Dobson

Editor: Matt Dobson (author of the Living With Purpose series and TBH—To Be Honest The Truth Will Set You Free: a Life Study for Teens)

All rights reserved. Except for pages that are marked with permission to reproduce, no part of this book may be reproduced in any form without permission in writing from the author, except in the case of brief quotations embodied in the text.

We hope you enjoy this book. Our goals are to provide insight into the twelve disciples, to give Biblical guidance on how to look up the disciples using the Bible, and understand how the disciples relate to us. Different versions of the Bible are at the user's discretion. We would like to recommend that a Bible with a Concordance be used with this Bible study.

CAMELLIA
HOUSE PUBLISHING

Camellia House Publishing, Century, FL
Printed in the United States of America.

the TWELVE outlaws
T.S. Dobson

CONTENTS

Introduction 9

THE APOSTLES

1. SIMON PETER..11
2. ANDREW..21
3. JAMES son of Zebedee..........................29
4. JOHN...37
5. PHILIP...45
6. BARTHOLOMEW....................................53
7. MATTHEW...61
8. THOMAS...69
9. JAMES the Less or Little......................77
10. SIMON the Zealot.................................85
11. THADDAEUS..91
12. JUDAS ISCARIOT...................................97

Plan of Salvation...105

How to make changes in your life..............107

Notes..109

To my children,
Hillary and Abby.

To my loving husband,
Matthew
for inspiring me.

Matthew 10:2-4 (NIV)

2These are the names of the twelve apostles: first, Simon (who is called Peter) and his brother Andrew; James son of Zebedee, and his brother John; 3Philip and Bartholomew; Thomas and Matthew the tax collector; James son of Alphaeus, and Thaddaeus; 4Simon the Zealot and Judas Iscariot, who betrayed him.

the TWELVE outlaws
T.S. Dobson

INTRODUCTION

It was a Friday afternoon as I headed to New Bethel. My Husband, Matt Dobson is pastor there and the church is called "the little white country church on the corner." It's located in the Florida panhandle in what is known as the New York Community. We were going to do some clean up that afternoon to prepare for Sunday worship. I had just completed earlier that summer a book for preteens called "The Fruit of the Spirit," and now I felt led by God to do another study for preteens and teens on the disciples of the Bible. I was thinking about my title and came up with many different ones, but something just didn't click on a good name for it. While driving to the church and with much prayer, God revealed to me that afternoon what the study would be called.

"WANTED!" That was it! Growing up I always loved watching those old black and white western movies. My dad loved them and I started watching them too. Many times the plot centered around catching someone who was considered an outlaw; wanted by a group for some law of the land they had broken, or some misunderstanding. So it made sense to me to name the title, "The TWELVE Outlaws." Why? Well I hope with this study you'll see why these disciples were "WANTED!"

And my hope is that you will have a better understanding of them and why Jesus chose them.

They were typical men: some were fishermen, tax collectors, and some were even political activists. Reading through the New Testament you'll find they were normal people you could relate to. Jesus came from Heaven to earth, but he didn't mind hanging out with an earthly crowd. If he can love that rugged bunch of outlaws from the Bible, surely we all have a chance.

God bless!

Matthew 28:19

Therefore go and make disciples of all nations, baptizing them in the name of the Father and of the Son and of the Holy Spirit.

Matthew 16:18
"And I tell you that you are Peter, and on this rock I will build my church, and the gates of Hades will not overcome it."

the FIRST outlaw

PETER—also known as Simon Peter

Meaning of his name: called Simon until Jesus Christ gave him the name Peter, which means "rock", or the greek word for rock "petros." The apostle of hope.

Apostle Profile

Father: Jonas (John 1:42)

Brother: Andrew (John 1:40)

Occupation: Fisherman and apostle of Jesus

Birth: Bethsaida in Galilee (John 1:44)

Death: Died in Rome

the TWELVE outlaws
T.S. Dobson

Why was Peter "WANTED!" by Christ?

⇒ **Christ loved Peter for his big heart.**

⇒ **Spokesman: Peter was bold and spoke his feelings.**

⇒ **Leader in the early church**

Background check: Peter's true name was Simon. His brother was Andrew. Simon was known as a follower of John the Baptist. Andrew introduced Simon to Jesus, at that time Jesus renamed Simon to Cephas, which means "rock." Peter was rough around the edges, but he was a man with a big heart and Jesus loved him. Sometimes Peter was known for letting his emotions get the best of him and that sometimes got him in trouble for being too bold. But being bold gave Peter the ability to be a good speaker for Christ and the other disciples. Peter, who was clearly one of the favorites of Jesus, was in Jesus' inner circle along with the other disciples James and John (Mark 5:35-43). Peter was also a witness to the transfiguration (Matt. 17:1-9). Those same three disciples saw the agony of Jesus in the Garden of Gethsemane (Mark 14:33-42).

Peter had two calls by Jesus. The first call brought no immediate change in Peter's life. He looked upon Jesus as his teacher, but no command yet to follow as a disciple. His second call came on the Sea of Galilee with Andrew, Peter, James, and John while fishing. The people wanted to hear from Jesus, so He got in Peter's boat and they went out a little from the land. He addressed the multitude, and the miracle of the fish happened. Shortly after, Jesus wanted time alone and sent the men out to sea, where a storm brewed and tossed the boat around. Read what happened next: Matthew 14: 22-33.

the TWELVE outlaws
T.S. Dobson

Peter's STRENGTHS:

He was a loyal man. Like many of the disciples of Jesus, he left his occupation to follow Christ for three years. Jesus taught him about the Kingdom of Heaven. Peter became a fierce and "on fire" missionary for Christ.

His WEAKNESSES:

Simon Peter knew great fear and doubt. He was known for breaking his promises. He was always the first to speak his mind, sometimes he would stick his foot in his mouth or walk right into a situation (walk on water) without thinking it all through. These weaknesses came from his lack of faith in God at certain times in his life.

His REWARD & ACHIEVEMENTS:

He was called by Jesus (Mt 4:18-20; Mk 1:16-20; Lk 5:10; Jn 1:40-42)

He witnessed Jesus Christ perform miracles (Mt. 8:14-15; Mk 1:30-31; Lk 4:38-39; Mt 17:24-27; Lk 5:4-8; Jn 21:2-6)

How can you relate and what can we learn from Peter's life?

"Open mouth, insert foot!!"

You could probably relate to Peter's personality in many ways. Always piping up and saying things before thinking it through. Sometimes speaking up is good, but it requires some forethought. I'm sure there have been times when you spoke too soon. Many times I have said something to quickly and it was too late to take the words back once spoken. You can try to put a bandage on it so-to-speak, but a bandage is just a bandage. It just covers up something that is still there, and in the end when you take the bandage off you still may have a scar from it. We can be harsh with our words and leave scars on friendships and even family members.

What about the time when Peter was excited about seeing Jesus walk on water? Peter tried it himself only to let doubt and panic cause him to sink. I'm sure you can relate to this when you get excited about God, and answered prayer. But when something happens and another prayer doesn't get answered; your faith may seem to fade and is not as strong as it once might have been.

God doesn't always answer every prayer the way we want Him to. We don't always understand why things happen to us. This can make us question our faith.

the TWELVE outlaws
T.S. Dobson

In time we might see the end results of why God maybe didn't answer a prayer like we hoped. God knows us best, and He also knows what's best for us. If we continue to BELIEVE and TRUST in Him, He will help us rise from the sinking waters that can overtake us in our life.

When we rise from the waters we realize how strong our faith has become. We see how God will answer our prayers when needed. Like Christ showed Peter, his greatness will save us from ourselves. When we trust Christ, we believe in him and what he has done for us. Go out and be a spokesman for Christ, and tell the world about God. Don't be ashamed and deny this truth. God will reward you for this. Fear and doubt can cause us to deny Christ to work in our lives. Let him carry us through the storms.

Point to ponder: Sometimes you might forget that **GOD IS IN CONTROL**, and by forgetting this all important fact, you overstep your limited authority, and lack in faith.

We can relate to Peter in many ways. It's hard for us to realize we aren't in control, or to give up our control because of pride. Just remember, without God's control, we have no control!

Why did Jesus restore Peter's favor as a disciple?

Peter was not perfect and was guilty of denying Christ. Even though Peter stumbled, he proved that he loved the Lord. After Jesus Christ's crucifixion, a humbled Peter and John went to the tomb. It was the morning of the resurrection and Jesus revealed Himself to them. On the shores of Galilee, the Lord asked Peter three times "Simon, son of Jonas, do you love me?" Simon Peter said "Yes." After this showing he restored Peter's faith and belief.

On the day of Pentecost, Peter, a spokesman of the apostles, preached an amazing sermon which resulted in 3,000 being saved for Christ.

Acts 10:34-35
Then Peter began to speak: "I now realize how true it is that God does not show favoritism but accepts men from every nation who fear him and do what is right."

Our personality can be like the shifting sands of time, but God wants us to become like granite. Solid in our walk with Him. Like a ROCK!

1 Peter 4:16
However, if you suffer as a Christian, do not be ashamed, but praise God that you bear that name.

the TWELVE outlaws
T.S. Dobson

Concordance Study Time:

Using a Bible with a concordance in the back, find 5 verses about PETER. Write them down below. Write the Book and verse number only. This will be a quick reference for you on the apostle Peter. Then go to those verses in the Bible and study them.

_____
_____
_____
_____
_____

Read the verses you jotted down above, then come up with your own version of what those verses mean to you. Study at least one of the verses you chose about the apostle Peter. If you don't understand a term in the verse, look it up in the dictionary so that you can relate to what the Bible is saying to you.

_____
_____
_____
_____
_____
_____

(This page may be reproduced to use in a bible study group.)

the TWELVE outlaws
T.S. Dobson

Question & Answer Response:

1. What did you learn about apostle Peter?

_____
_____
_____
_____

2. Name a strength and a weakness of Peter?

_____
_____
_____
_____

3. Can you name an experience in your life where you can relate to Peter?

_____
_____
_____
_____

Prayer Time:

Lord, thank you for teaching me about the Apostle Peter. Help me to be like Peter and put my faith and trust in you. Help me show others my love for you and to not be afraid or fear being a follower of Christ. I ask these things in Jesus name. Amen.

(This page may be reproduced to use in a bible study group.)

John 1:41
Andrew went to find his brother, Simon, and told him, "We have found the Messiah" (which means "Christ").

the SECOND outlaw

ANDREW

Meaning of his name: manly; brave. The apostle of small things.

Apostle Profile

Father: Jonas (John 1:42)

Brother: Peter (John 1:40; Matthew 4:18)

Occupation: Fisherman and apostle (Mark 1:16)

Birth: Bethsaida in Galilee (John 1:44)

Death: Martyred in Greece.

the TWELVE outlaws
T.S. Dobson

Why was Andrew **"WANTED!"** by Christ?

⇒ He was deliberate, bold, and decisive.

⇒ He saw the value and good in the small things.

Background check: Andrew was the first disciple to be called by Jesus. Andrew was very close to Jesus, thoughtful, and strong in his faith. Like many apostles he was a fisherman, which of course required physical strength. Andrew was known for bringing others to meet Christ. He was even responsible for bringing his older brother, Peter, to Christ. He was not as popular as the other disciples in the lead group. Andrew wasn't one to be up in the front crowd, but rather in the back making small differences for Christ. He appreciated the value of bringing just one person to Christ. He had a different style from Peter. As you read earlier, Peter didn't mind being bold. He would speak to thousands in a crowd. Andrew's style was to speak one-on-one to others about Jesus. Since it was Andrew who brought Peter to Christ, they both were accountable for spreading the gospel to thousands.

Andrew didn't expect a pat on the back for bringing others to Christ. He didn't need to be the center of attention. Jesus knew of his contribution to the ministry because he was so close to Andrew. Andrew was present when Jesus was baptized and heard John the Baptist say, "Behold the lamb of God!" (John 1:35-36).

the TWELVE outlaws
T.S. Dobson

👉 Andrew's **STRENGTHS:**

He always strived for the truth. As a follower, first of John the Baptist, and then Jesus Christ, he sought the truth. He was thoughtful in his approach to the ministry. He was non-confrontational. He liked to stay in the background, to get a different perspective from the other leaders. Because he would take a step back to look at the whole picture, he became a good leader. He was more approachable, and less impulsive than some of the other disciples. Andrew gave hope to others.

👉 His **WEAKNESSES:**

Andrew abandoned Jesus during his trial and crucifixion. (John 18:15)

👉 His **REWARD & ACHIEVEMENTS:**

Andrew brought people to Jesus. He became a missionary like many of the other followers of Christ and preached the gospel.

Andrew brought a boy with two fish and five barley loaves to Jesus, who then multiplied them to feed 5,000 people (John 6:8-13).

the TWELVE outlaws
T.S. Dobson

How can you relate to Andrew?

There have been times that I have helped others without taking credit for it. I'm sure you know people who like to be the center of attention, and sometimes we probably like it ourselves. This can boost our confidence, but sometimes this can make us prideful. Too much attention can cause us to be boastful.

As a result from Andrew's life, we can learn to appreciate the small contributions. What you do matters!

Like playing in a game, all the players have positions that our important. Even though one position might get more spotlight, the game can't be played without all contributions of the team members. My daughter Hillary plays point guard in basketball. She would tell you without hesitation that each players position is important. And as a track and cross country coach, I realize it takes a team of runners and a coach to train them to win a meet.

Andrew and the other disciples were on a team; a team for Jesus. Some disciples had smaller parts like Andrew, but they are all important! Jesus is like the coach, training his athletes to win. To win souls for Christ!

the TWELVE outlaws
T.S. Dobson

What can we learn from Andrew's life?

Andrew's legacy teaches us that it's often the little things that count, the small gifts and talents, and the quiet voice that can sometimes reach the most. You never know which person might be the next big evangelist like Andrew's brother Peter.

Andrew may not have preached to thousand's like his brother, but one-by-one he led people to Christ. For example, he brought a little boy to Jesus with five pieces of bread and two fish. Jesus listened to Andrew and took the small food this boy had and multiplied it to feed thousands. You never have to feel insufficient when you bring all you have to Jesus. He will take your little and increase its effectiveness.

Unlike the others disciples who felt they would have to send the mass of people away to get food for themselves, Andrew had faith that Jesus would supply people with their needs. That took true faith!

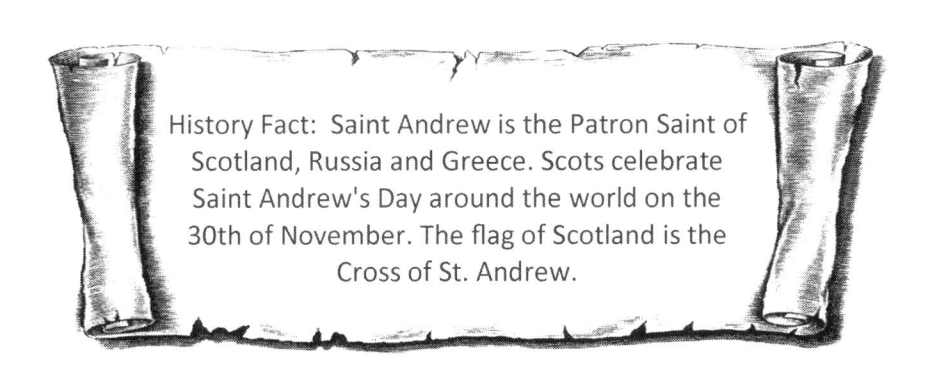

History Fact: Saint Andrew is the Patron Saint of Scotland, Russia and Greece. Scots celebrate Saint Andrew's Day around the world on the 30th of November. The flag of Scotland is the Cross of St. Andrew.

the TWELVE outlaws
T.S. Dobson

Concordance Study Time:

Using a Bible with a concordance in the back, find 5 verses about ANDREW. Write them down below. Write the Book and verse number only. This will be a quick reference for you on the apostle Andrew. Then go to those verses in the Bible and study them.

_____
_____
_____
_____
_____

Read the verses you jotted down above, then come up with your own version of what those verses mean to you. Study at least one of the verses you chose about the apostle Andrew. If you don't understand a term in the verse, look it up in the dictionary so that you can relate to what the Bible is saying to you.

_____
_____
_____
_____
_____
_____
_____

(This page may be reproduced to use in a bible study group.)

the TWELVE outlaws
T.S. Dobson

Question & Answer Response:

1. What did you learn about apostle Andrew?

_____
_____
_____
_____

2. Name a strength and a weakness of Andrew?

_____
_____
_____
_____

3. Can you name an experience in your life where you can relate to Andrew?

_____
_____
_____
_____

Prayer Time:

Lord, thank you for teaching me about the Apostle Andrew. Help me to be like Andrew and go out and make a difference. Help me to appreciate that even the smallest act of sharing your love to others counts. I ask these things in Jesus name. Amen.

(This page may be reproduced to use in a bible study group.)

Matthew 20:23
Jesus said to them, "You will indeed drink from my cup, but to sit at my right or left is not for me to grant. These places belong to those for whom they have been prepared by my Father."

the THIRD outlaw

JAMES

Meaning of his name: "heel catcher." Both he and his brother John were nicknamed "Boanerges" by Christ, which meant "Sons of Thunder" (Mark 3:17). The apostle of passion.

Apostle Profile

Father: Zebedee (Matthew 4:21)

Mother: Salome (Mark 15:40)

Brother: John (Matthew 4:21)

Occupation: Fisherman, one of Jesus key three apostles

Birth: Bethsaida in Galilee

Death: Killed by sword (Acts 12:2)

the TWELVE outlaws
T.S. Dobson

👉 James' STRENGTHS:

James was a loyal disciple of Jesus. His qualities were outstanding and his character made him one of Jesus' favorites.

👉 His WEAKNESSES:

Sometimes James was considered brash, quick to think, and sometimes impulsive. Sometimes he took earthly matters into his own hands and didn't apply Divine guidance.

👉 His REWARD & ACHIEVEMENTS:

James followed Jesus as his disciple and was honored in a favored position. He was one of three chosen to be in Jesus' inner circle along with his brother John, and also Simon Peter. These three chosen ones were invited by Jesus to witness events that others didn't get to see: daughter of Jairus being raised from the dead (Mark 5:37-47); the transfiguration (Matthew 17:1-3); and Jesus' agony in the Garden of Gethsemane (Matthew 26-36-37).

the TWELVE outlaws
T.S. Dobson

Why was James **"WANTED!"** by Christ?

⇒ **James was passionate, fervent, thunderous.**

⇒ **He also had an ambitious drive.**

Background check: James was probably the oldest of the two brothers as he was mentioned primarily first in the Bible. James and his brother John, who you will read about later, were fishermen with their father Zebedee on the Sea of Galilee. They left their trade of fishing to follow Jesus.

Although his traits of being considered ambitious sometimes got the best of James, he had a zealous and passionate nature. We see this in Luke 9:51-56 when James wanted to call down fire from Heaven.

Like his brother James wanted to be able to sit on both sides of the throne in God's Kingdom. Jesus quickly reminded them that it would take some suffering before such a glory could be given and that those thrones were in God's hands. Read what Jesus Christ said to them in Matthew 20:23.

James was the first of the disciples to be martyred, or killed. He was killed with the sword on order of King Herod of Judea, about 44 A.D. (Acts 12:1-2)

No doubt James was a loyal disciple of Jesus!

👉 How can you relate and what can we learn from James' life?

Passion! It's a powerful thing to possess. Passion can be good or bad. James had a misguided passion, before Christ came into his life. But when Jesus entered his life, he took the gift of passion James had and used it for the good.

Passion and ambition go together. Passion is having the drive to do something and ambition is putting it in place.

You can relate to James' passion because of your own sense of passion. Worldly passion or unworldly passion? Worldly passion can cause us to become jealous or envious. It can cause us to idolize material things and relationships. Having a passion to spend money can lead to an addiction.

Passion can also be used for good. You can have a passion for sports; which promotes teamwork. You can have a passion to use a talent or gift you've been given. For example; singing, creating art, or speaking in front of others. You can use passion for the good. A higher call is to use your passion for Christ. Take the talent or gift you have and use it to passionately spread the gospel like the apostle James.

the TWELVE outlaws
T.S. Dobson

As believers in Christ, sometimes we expect things to be given to us when we do good for others. We like an answered prayer for the good we do. James, as a follower of Christ, had high expectations of where he wanted to be. He liked to be ranked high for the good he had done. But Christ reminded him many times that goodness had to be earned and not just given. James wanted the glory, but Jesus told him he must first go through worldly suffering. James wanted great power, but Jesus showed him that humbleness was the way to glory.

There are times when it is hard to let go of our idolized material possessions, and exchange it for something much greater.

Worldly suffering can be caused by unbelievers throughout your life, but you must stand up for your beliefs. God takes in account all that you do to glorify His name. To lift him up high in your heart is where He wants to be. Serving Him is the key, whether its in great or small ways. You must look for the passion of Christ!

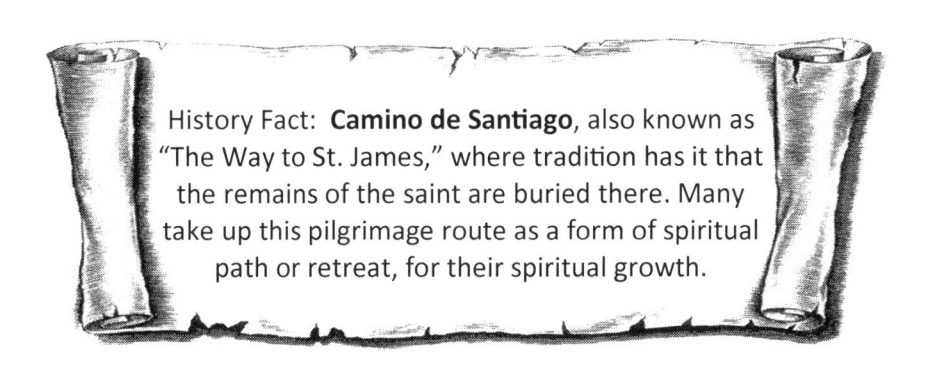

History Fact: **Camino de Santiago**, also known as "The Way to St. James," where tradition has it that the remains of the saint are buried there. Many take up this pilgrimage route as a form of spiritual path or retreat, for their spiritual growth.

the TWELVE outlaws
T.S. Dobson

Concordance Study Time:

Using a Bible with a concordance in the back, find 5 verses about JAMES. Write them down below. Write the Book and verse number only. This will be a quick reference for you on the apostle James. Then go to those verses in the Bible and study them.

_____
_____
_____
_____
_____

Read the verses you jotted down above, then come up with your own version of what those verses mean to you. Study at least one of the verses you chose about the apostle James. If you don't understand a term in the verse, look it up in the dictionary so that you can relate to what the Bible is saying to you.

_____
_____
_____
_____
_____
_____
_____

(This page may be reproduced to use in a bible study group.)

Question & Answer Response:

1. What did you learn about apostle James?

_____
_____
_____
_____

2. Name a strength and a weakness of James?

_____
_____
_____
_____

3. Can you name an experience in your life where you can relate to James?

_____
_____
_____
_____

Prayer Time:

Lord, thank you for teaching me about the Apostle James. Help me to be like James and show that I have passion to spread your word, to be bold. Help me to be ambitious to learn your word through reading the Bible. I ask these things in Jesus name. Amen.

(This page may be reproduced to use in a bible study group.)

1 John 4:16-17
And so we know and rely on the love God has for us. God is love. Whoever lives in loves lives in God, and God in him.

the FOURTH outlaw

JOHN

Meaning of his name: "Grace of Jehovah"
Like his brother James both were nicknamed "Boanerges" by Christ, which meant, "Sons of Thunder". (Mark 3:17) The apostle of love.

Apostle Profile

Father: Zebedee (Matthew 4:21)

Mother: Salome (Mark 15:40)

Brother: James (Matthew 4:21)

Occupation: Fisherman and one of Jesus key three disciples

Birth: Bethsaida in Galilee

Death: Died in Ephesus.

the TWELVE outlaws
T.S. Dobson

👉 John's STRENGTHS:

John was loyal to Christ. He was the only one of the 12 apostles (disciples) present at the cross when Jesus died. John went out like Peter and spoke boldly preaching the gospel in Jerusalem where he suffered many beatings and imprisonment for doing so. He saw Jesus' unconditional love and preached this same love to others.

👉 His WEAKNESSES:

Like James he was quick to judge others and call down fire upon unbelievers (Luke 9:51-56). He also asked for a favored position in the kingdom of heaven.

👉 His REWARD & ACHIEVEMENTS:

John was one of the first disciples chosen. He wrote the Gospel of John; 1, 2, and 3. He was an elder of the early church spreading the gospel message. Jesus entrusted John with the care of His own mother.

the TWELVE outlaws
T.S. Dobson

Why was John "**WANTED!**" by Christ?

⇒ **Love for Christ.**

⇒ **Like his brother James, he was zealous, passionate, thunderous, showed humility and ambition.**

Background check: John was considered the one who wrote about love more than any other New Testament author. He was a beloved friend of Christ. He was considered a pillar of strength in the early church. His brother was James, another fishermen on the Sea of Galilee. He, like his brother James and Peter, were apart of Jesus' inner circle. They saw the miracle of Jairus' daughter being raised from the dead, the transfiguration, and Jesus' agony in the Garden of Gethsemane. He tried to call fire down from heaven on a village that rejected Jesus Christ.

John served in Jerusalem in the early church for many years. He used many symbols as titles for Christ, such as the Lamb of God (John 1:29), the vine (John 15:5), and the resurrection (John 20).

John doesn't speak of himself in the Books of John as John, but more frequently as the apostle with whom Jesus loved. Make no mistake that John's passion for truth was based on the love of Christ. John saw the suffering that Christ endured, and this made John an even stronger apostle. He saw Jesus' suffering on the cross. John himself endured suffering for his beliefs, like many in the early church of apostles.

After the crucifixion, Christ revealed himself to John and Peter at the Sea of Galilee. He was the first disciple to run to the tomb after Jesus' resurrection. In the book of John, John regarded himself as the "disciple whom Jesus loved."

the TWELVE outlaws
T.S. Dobson

How can you relate and what can we learn from John's life?

Love is the number one fruit of the Holy Spirit and it's what John was known for. He cultivated his love for Christ. John emphasized the truth that is found in the gospel. John wrote the following.

3 John 4
"I have no greater joy than to hear that my children walk in truth."

In his gospel, John wrote the word *truth* dozens of times. As written in Mark 9:39-40, John learned the balance between truth and love. Read in the Bible to understand how this happened. John was transformed at that time. In Mark 10:35-37, John learned to balance his ambition and humility when he requested to sit on the throne near God. Jesus had to correct him. John learned respect for authority, and work was required to be a part of the kingdom of heaven. Nothing was just given freely. John suffered for his beliefs on earth. The glory he would receive would be far greater. Witnessing the transfiguration and walking with Christ helped him understand the balance of ambition and humility.

So how do we relate? John showed love for Christ. When others see us show love in our actions they see us as different. But this difference isn't a bad thing, and when others see that you show love and kindness they will know something is genuinely different about you; a good thing! People are usually attracted to things that are loving and happy. They may ask why you are this way and this will open a door for conversation about Christ.

the TWELVE outlaws
T.S. Dobson

When we look at John's life we see him learn a balance between love and truth, ambition and humility, and suffering and glory. When we are learning more and more about Christ we realize that their must be a balance in our lives between what the Bible has to say and our daily actions. If we are living for Christ we will want to read the truths from the Bible and apply it to our lives based on our love for others. We will want to be ambitious and spread the gospel, but yet also show humility to those who still have yet to believe. To be patient in our walk with Christ, it's likely will be patient with others. In the early church, many apostles suffered for their belief in Jesus. It's not much different today than the early church. Many times we are ridiculed for believing in a Savior that freed us from our sin and the gates of hell. It's a suffering like John experienced. In the end, his expressions of love showed others about Jesus. John had security in his beliefs, and knew where he would spend eternity after he left this world.

If you are struggling with the truth of who Christ is you can read about him through the books of John. John gives eyewitness accounts for Christ. He also saw the glory of Christ resurrection, and wants to spread the news to you! You can know love and truth too. Pray for this balance in your life.

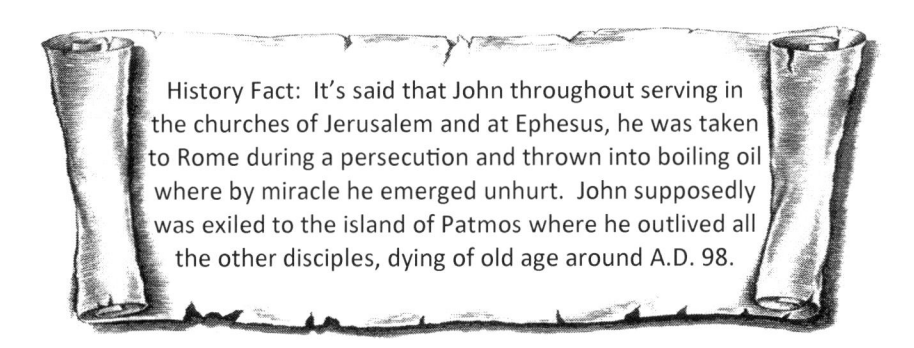

> History Fact: It's said that John throughout serving in the churches of Jerusalem and at Ephesus, he was taken to Rome during a persecution and thrown into boiling oil where by miracle he emerged unhurt. John supposedly was exiled to the island of Patmos where he outlived all the other disciples, dying of old age around A.D. 98.

the TWELVE outlaws
T.S. Dobson

Concordance Study Time:

Using a Bible with a concordance in the back, find 5 verses about JOHN. Write them down below. Write the Book and verse number only. This will be a quick reference for you on the apostle John. Then go to those verses in the Bible and study them.

_____
_____
_____
_____
_____

Read the verses you jotted down above, then come up with your own version of what those verses mean to you. Study at least one of the verses you chose about the apostle John. If you don't understand a term in the verse, look it up in the dictionary so that you can relate to what the Bible is saying to you.

_____
_____
_____
_____
_____
_____

(This page may be reproduced to use in a bible study group.)

the TWELVE outlaws
T.S. Dobson

Question & Answer Response:

1. What did you learn about apostle John?

_____
_____
_____
_____

2. Name a strength and a weakness of John?

_____
_____
_____
_____

3. Can you name an experience in your life where you can relate to John?

_____
_____
_____
_____

Prayer Time:

Lord, thank you for teaching me about the Apostle John. Help me to be like John and show love to others. Help me to not be afraid or fear being a follower of Christ and look to the Bible for truth. I ask these things in Jesus name. Amen.

(This page may be reproduced to use in a bible study group.)

John 1:45
Philip found Nathanael and told him, "We have found the one Moses wrote about in the Law, and about whom the prophets also wrote — Jesus of Nazareth, the son of Joseph."

the FIFTH outlaw

PHILIP—The bean counter; also known as "curious" by the other apostles.

Meaning of his name: "Lover of horses"

Apostle Profile

Occupation: Apostle

Birth: Bethsaida, Galilean Sea

Death: Died at Hierapolis, a city near Colosse and Laodicia

the TWELVE outlaws
T.S. Dobson

👉 Philip's **STRENGTHS**:

Philip sought for answers; recognizing Jesus as the promised Savior.

👉 His **WEAKNESSES**:

Like the other apostles, Philip was a deserter during Jesus' trial and crucifixion. He did not fully understand the gospel until Jesus' resurrection. He questioned Jesus about God the Father, and wanted to see evidence. He had lack of faith at times.

👉 His **REWARD & ACHIEVEMENTS**:

Philip learned the truth of the gospel at Jesus feet. He learned about the Kingdom of God and preached about Jesus' resurrection and ascension.

the TWELVE outlaws
T.S. Dobson

Why was Philip **"WANTED!"** by Christ?

⇒ **Jesus knew he had a weak faith.**

⇒ **He was an administrator and leader.**

Background check: Jesus called upon Philip saying, "Follow me." (John 1:43) Even though Philip was known to be pessimistic or negative at times, and sometimes cynical, Jesus still wanted him. Philip was considered a leader of the second group of four disciples. He had a distinct character, but was different from Peter, Andrew, James, and John. Philip studied about Jesus and the law. He had been preparing himself for Jesus, who was called the Messiah.

Philip followed Jesus, based on the fulfillment of the Old Testament promises. He struggled with a weak faith as seen in John 6:5-7.

When Jesus looked up and saw a great crowd coming toward him, he said to Philip, "Where shall we buy bread for these people to eat?" He asked this only to test him, for he already had in mind what he was going to do. Philip answered him, "It would take more than half a year's wages to buy enough bread for each one to have a bite!"

Philip was thinking negatively about the situation when he didn't consider what Jesus could do as the Messiah. If he had put all his faith in Jesus he would have told Jesus, "Lord, you can feed them, I'm just going to watch and learn from you." But instead, he was weak, and thinking only of what he could see or rationalize. He could have responded like Andrew did, mentioning a boy who was near with food, and then Jesus could have multiplied the food. Philip saw of this miracle and believed.

the TWELVE outlaws
T.S. Dobson

> How can you relate and what can we learn from Philip's life?

"But Jesus said, "He's exactly what I'm looking for. My strength is made perfect in weakness." Jesus made Philip into a preacher, and led him to become one of the early Church founders.

Philip learned a lesson in faith when Jesus fed the multitudes. Although Philip had lost a great opportunity to answer Jesus with great faith, Jesus showed him that, *"If you have faith as a mustard seed, you will say to this mountain, "Move from here to there," and it will move; and nothing will be impossible for you"* (Matthew 17:20). Even though Philip was traditional in his approach to feeding the multitude; Jesus used this instance to show him how faith works.

Philip had lessons to learn. Because Philip relied too much on his own understanding he had to learn how to strengthen his faith. Thankfully, the Lord uses people like Philip, as a testimony of how people grow in the Holy Spirit.

Philip along with other disciples made some pretty ignorant statements. One other instance for Philip was in John 14:8-9.

> *Philip said, "Lord, show us the Father and that will be enough for us." Jesus answered: "Don't you know me, Philip, even after I have been among you such a long time? Anyone who has seen me has seen the father. How can you say, 'Show us the Father'?"*

Philip searched for the path to salvation and found it in Jesus Christ. He learned that Eternal life is available to anyone who desires it.

the TWELVE outlaws
T.S. Dobson

How can we relate?

First, let's talk about why he struggled with being negative or pessimistic. In this day and age, it's hard to see the positive in negative situations. There are some things we can't control and situations with family and friends challenge us everyday. You may have heard of someone say, "You get up on the wrong side of the bed." This phrase means starting our day with the wrong attitude. We might wake up with negative thoughts going through our mind, but we can control our negativity and turn our day around. Pray when you wake up. Pray that God will give you grace and a positive attitude to face the day!

Secondly, let's talk about his lack of faith. Philip had a small faith, so Jesus chose to refine him through all the testings of his faith. It worked and Philip's faith got stronger. When you go through tough times and it seems you are alone, believe that God is there for you. **"If He brings you to it, by faith He will bring you through it!"**

Thirdly, due to Philip's lack of faith, he was cynical, meaning he was motivated by his own interests. We need to put our faith in God, not in worldly things. Putting your faith in worldly things will only lead to disappointment. Pray God gives you wisdom to make the right choices!

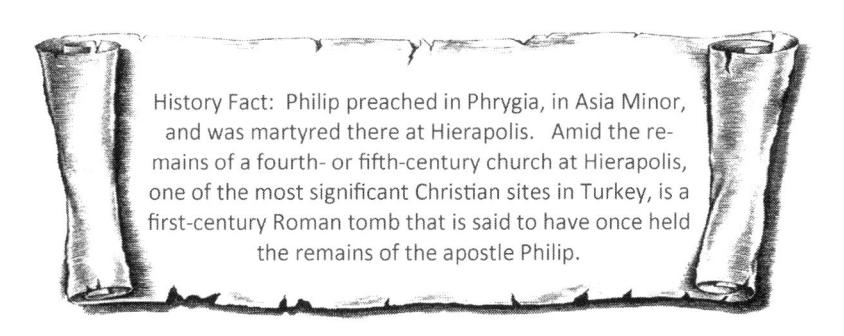

History Fact: Philip preached in Phrygia, in Asia Minor, and was martyred there at Hierapolis. Amid the remains of a fourth- or fifth-century church at Hierapolis, one of the most significant Christian sites in Turkey, is a first-century Roman tomb that is said to have once held the remains of the apostle Philip.

the TWELVE outlaws
T.S. Dobson

Concordance Study Time:

Using a Bible with a concordance in the back, find 5 verses about PHILIP. Write them down below. Write the Book and verse number only. This will be a quick reference for you on the apostle Philip. Then go to those verses in the Bible and study them.

_____
_____
_____
_____
_____

Read the verses you jotted down above, then come up with your own version of what those verses mean to you. Study at least one of the verses you chose about the apostle Philip. If you don't understand a term in the verse, look it up in the dictionary so that you can relate to what the Bible is saying to you.

_____
_____
_____
_____
_____
_____

(This page may be reproduced to use in a bible study group.)

the TWELVE outlaws
T.S. Dobson

Question & Answer Response:

1. What did you learn about apostle Philip?

_____
_____
_____
_____

2. Name a strength and a weakness of Philip?

_____
_____
_____
_____

3. Can you name an experience in your life where you can relate to Philip?

_____
_____
_____
_____

Prayer Time:

Lord, thank you for teaching me about the Apostle Philip. Help me to be like Philip and walk in faith. Help me show others a positive attitude, and not be self-centered, but be Christ centered. I ask these things in Jesus name. Amen.

(This page may be reproduced to use in a bible study group.)

John 1:47
"Behold, an Israelite indeed, in whom is no deceit!"

the SIXTH outlaw

BARTHOLOMEW—also known as Nathanael

Meaning of his name: "Gift of God"; family designation meaning "son of Tolmai."

Apostle Profile

Occupation: Apostle

Birth: Cana of Galilee

Death: City of Alban

the TWELVE outlaws
T.S. Dobson

👉 Bartholomew's STRENGTHS:

Nathanael Bartholomew was pure in his heart. He desired truth. He overcame his skepticism about Nazareth. He left his past behind.

👉 His WEAKNESSES:

He suffered from personal prejudices and judging.

👉 His REWARD & ACHIEVEMENTS:

Like many of the disciples he abandoned Jesus during his trial and crucifixion.

the TWELVE outlaws
T.S. Dobson

Why was Bartholomew **"WANTED!"** by Christ?

⇒ **Nathanael Bartholomew was pure of heart.**

⇒ **He desired to know truth.**

Background check: Most scholars believe that Nathanael and Bartholomew were one in the same. There's not much background about Bartholomew. We know that Bartholomew was brought to Jesus after Philip. Bartholomew's call came after Jesus saw him sitting under a fig tree. John describes the calling of Bartholomew in John 1:46-51.

46 "Nazareth!" exclaimed Nathanael. "Can anything good come from Nazareth?" "Come and see for yourself," Philip replied. 47 As they approached, Jesus said, "Now here is a genuine son of Israel—a man of complete integrity." 48 "How do you know about me?" Nathanael asked. Jesus replied, "I could see you under the fig tree before Philip found you." 49 Then Nathanael exclaimed, "Rabbi, you are the Son of God—the King of Israel!" 50 Jesus asked him, "Do you believe this just because I told you I had seen you under the fig tree? You will see greater things than this." 51 Then he said, "I tell you the truth, you will all see heaven open and the angels of God going up and down on the Son of Man, the one who is the stairway between heaven and earth."

In this scripture we get a glimpse of Bartholomew's beliefs. Bartholomew was seeking truth and he knew he believed in God and longed to receive the Messiah. It took a long time to understand who Christ was, Nathanael Bartholomew's faith in Jesus was affirmed. Jesus of course already knew Bartholomew's heart.

# the TWELVE outlaws
T.S. Dobson

How can you relate and what can we learn from Bartholomew's life?

His response to Jesus being from Nazareth, showed a deep prejudice. He said it was based on sheer emotion and bigotry. He had an inward hate for the whole town of Nazareth. Fortunately, his prejudice against Nazareth didn't stop him from seeking the truth. He saught the truth and when Philip said, "Come and see,"; he went. Once he finally met Jesus, he quickly changed his attitude about being prejudice towards Nazareth.

What a great moment for Bartholomew to hear these words from Christ at the moment he was seeking to hear the truth found in John 1:47.

"Behold, an Israelite indeed, in whom is no deceit!"

Jesus had seen Bartholomew through an omniscient eye, and he knew his heart was pure despite having been prejudice. Jesus knew Bart didn't have a false character. John 2:25 describes Jesus thoughts:

"and needed no one to bear witness about man, for he himself knew what was in man."

Matthew 5:8 says,

"Blessed are the pure in heart, for they will see God."

Sometimes our personal prejudice or a preconceived opinion can cause us to judge others. Bartholomew learned that being opened to God's word, will help you know the truth.

the TWELVE outlaws
T.S. Dobson

Jesus said it is not our place to judge, it is God's place. The best thing to do in a situation when it comes to hearing gossip is to pray for that person or situation and leave it in God's hands. He knows our hearts, and if we find ourselves showing prejudice we should pray.

Prejudice is ugly and sometimes we are at fault for showing it. A Christian should be prejudice-free. God defines it best in

1 John 4:8.

> Who does not love does not know God, because God is love.

God sees our hearts even when we mess up. He wants us to recognize when we are unfair toward a group of people. When we recognize or fault and correct it, we become closer in our walk with the Holy Spirit.

Have the "**W.W.J.D.** (What Would Jesus Do) Attitude!"

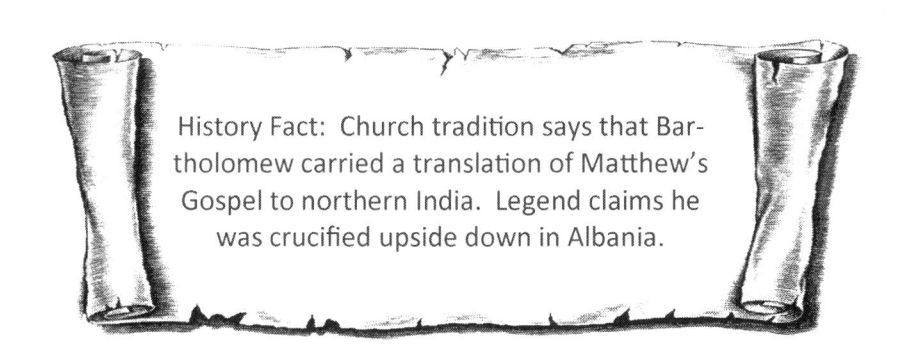

> History Fact: Church tradition says that Bartholomew carried a translation of Matthew's Gospel to northern India. Legend claims he was crucified upside down in Albania.

the TWELVE outlaws
T.S. Dobson

Concordance Study Time:

Using a Bible with a concordance in the back, find 5 verses about BARTHOLOMEW. Write them down below. Write the Book and verse number only. This will be a quick reference for you on the apostle Bartholomew. Then go to those verses in the Bible and study them.

_____
_____
_____
_____
_____

Read the verses you jotted down above, then come up with your own version of what those verses mean to you. Study at least one of the verses you chose about the apostle Bartholomew. If you don't understand a term in the verse, look it up in the dictionary so that you can relate to what the Bible is saying to you.

_____
_____
_____
_____
_____
_____
_____

(This page may be reproduced to use in a bible study group.)

though
the TWELVE outlaws
T.S. Dobson

Question & Answer Response:

1. What did you learn about apostle Bartholomew?

_____
_____
_____
_____

2. Name a strength and a weakness of Bartholomew?

_____
_____
_____
_____

3. Can you name an experience in your life where you can relate to Bartholomew?

_____
_____
_____
_____

Prayer Time:

Lord, thank you for teaching me about the Apostle Bartholomew. Help me to be like Bartholomew and seek truth. Help me show others my love for you and not to show prejudice or judge. I ask these things in Jesus name. Amen.

(This page may be reproduced to use in a bible study group.)

Matthew 9:9
As Jesus went on from there, he saw a man named Matthew sitting at the tax collector's booth. "Follow me," he told him, and Matthew got up and followed him.

the SEVENTH outlaw

MATTHEW

Meaning of his name: "Gift of God"

His original name was Levi. Matthew is shortened from the name Matthias.

Apostle Profile

Father: Alphaeus (Mark 2:14)

Brother: James the less (one of the 12 apostles)

Occupation: Tax collector then became an apostle (Matthew 9:9, 10:3)

Birth: Capernaum, a Galilean City (Matthew 9:1, 9)

Death: Died in Ethiopia

Matthew's **STRENGTHS:**

Matthew was an accurate record keeper and accountant. Once he committed to Jesus he served him with 100% loyalty. He knew of the human heart and the desires of the Jewish people.

His **WEAKNESSES:**

He was greedy before Jesus entered his life. He thought money was the most important thing on earth and violated God's laws at the expense of his countrymen. Neglecting the needs of the people and their state of welfare.

His **REWARD & ACHIEVEMENTS:**

He was a chosen disciple. Because Matthew was good with details he recorded an account of Jesus' life, his birth, his message and many of the deeds that were told in the Gospel of Matthew.

Matthew was a missionary for Christ; spreading the word to other countries.

… the **TWELVE** outlaws
T.S. Dobson

Why was Matthew "**WANTED!**" by Christ?

⇒ **He was a good record keeper.**

⇒ **He knew of the human heart and loyalty.**

Background check: Matthew wrote the Gospel of Matthew in the Bible. He was a tax collector. Tax collectors in Biblical days were considered dishonest and greedy. In other words, despicable scoundrels. The first time Matthew is mentioned is in a tax booth in Capernaum; collecting tax duty on imported goods brought by farmers and merchants, as well as others. Matthew paid all of the citizens taxes in advance, then he would charge the citizens more by raising the amount originally owed. This was for personal gain and greed. Matthew like most tax collectors had his own personal poesy of Roman soldiers to keep order and make people pay up.

We find that in his career as tax collector he was searching for answers; something more. He knew in his heart it was wrong and felt guilty for the greed, but continued in this sin until Jesus came into the picture. He was accountable for peoples money, and had heard of Jesus and who he claimed to be. He was spiritually hungry to know more about Jesus and what he had heard about him. Jesus knew his heart so he came to Matthew and said in Matthew 9:9.

"Follow Me."

Matthew was in the streets of Capernaum at a booth when Jesus approached him. With all the longing Matthew had to meet Jesus it didn't take him long to respond to Jesus. He dropped everything and went with him. He threw a feast in the city for people to meet the Messiah.

the TWELVE outlaws
T.S. Dobson

☞ How can you relate and what can we learn from Matthew's life?

Matthew was like a wealthy business man of today, or think of it as someone in the old west who owned all the bank money. He had control over the wealthy and the poor. But with all the wealth and greed no happiness was found from it. He knew there was something missing. Matthew's tortured soul had been looking for answers. He knew he was a Jew and he loved the Old Testament.

For the rest of his life, he served Jesus and went as a missionary to spread the law of God. He became a humble man who cared for all; from the wealthy to the poor of society. From this point on, instead of collecting taxes, Matthew was on a mission to collect souls for Jesus Christ.

Jesus knew even though Matthew was despised he could use him to spread the gospel to the Jews. Matthew was a qualified disciple because of his record keeping ability and he was a good observer of people and their character. Matthew was a detailed driven person.

Matthew 22: 37-39
37 Jesus replied: "'Love the Lord your God with all your heart and with all your soul and with all your mind.' 38 This is the first and greatest commandment. 39 And the second is like it: 'Love your neighbor as yourself.'

the TWELVE outlaws
T.S. Dobson

Matthew stands as a reminder that the Lord chooses the most despicable people of this world, changes them, and gives them a new heart to use in great ways. God can use anyone.

God wants to use you!

This teaches us that no person is unqualified because of lack of education, looks, or even their dirty rotten past. What Jesus wants is our commitment to him. He promises us a great reward for it! No matter what the world says you can and can't do; we don't have to be rich, have fame, or power to be a follower of Christ.

Matthew dropped his riches and power of this world to be a missionary for Christ. Heavenly power is much greater than the worldly power that is fleeting. Power and riches can't give us true happiness, but the power of the Holy Spirit in Christ can.

Write your story for Christ like the gospel of Matthew. Use your gifts like Matthew did for true spiritual growth. Follow the longing for Christ!

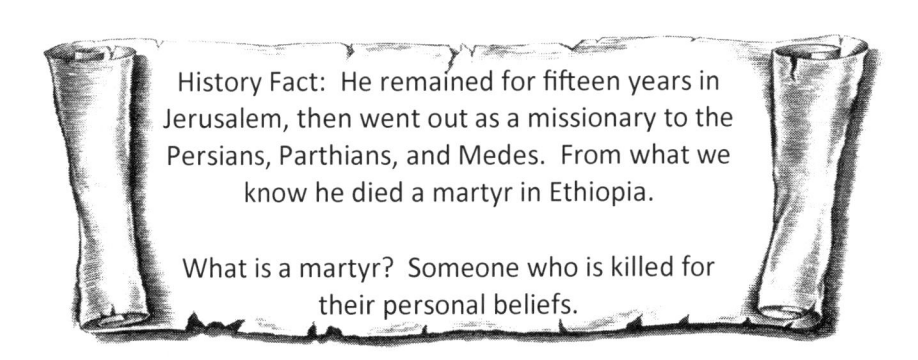

> History Fact: He remained for fifteen years in Jerusalem, then went out as a missionary to the Persians, Parthians, and Medes. From what we know he died a martyr in Ethiopia.
>
> What is a martyr? Someone who is killed for their personal beliefs.

the TWELVE outlaws
T.S. Dobson

Concordance Study Time:

Using a Bible with a concordance in the back, find 5 verses about MATTHEW. Write them down below. Write the Book and verse number only. This will be a quick reference for you on the apostle Matthew. Then go to those verses in the Bible and study them.

_____
_____
_____
_____
_____

Read the verses you jotted down above, then come up with your own version of what those verses mean to you. Study at least one of the verses you chose about the apostle Matthew. If you don't understand a term in the verse, look it up in the dictionary so that you can relate to what the Bible is saying to you.

_____
_____
_____
_____
_____
_____

(This page may be reproduced to use in a bible study group.)

the TWELVE outlaws
T.S. Dobson

Question & Answer Response:

1. What did you learn about apostle Matthew?

_____

_____

_____

_____

2. Name a strength and a weakness of Matthew?

_____

_____

_____

_____

3. Can you name an experience in your life where you can relate to Matthew?

_____

_____

_____

_____

Prayer Time:

Lord, thank you for teaching me about the Apostle Matthew. Help me to be like Matthew and put my trust in you Lord. Help me put you above all material riches and worldly things. I ask these things in Jesus name. Amen.

(This page may be reproduced to use in a bible study group.)

2 Corinthians 5:7
For we live by faith, not by sight.

the EIGHTH outlaw

THOMAS the Doubter

Meaning of his name: "twin" (Greek); Didymus also means "twin" (Aramaic)

Apostle Profile

Brother: Had an unnamed twin brother (John 11:16, 20:24, 21:2)

Occupation: Apostle

Birth: Area of Galilee

Death: Died in India

the TWELVE outlaws
T.S. Dobson

👉 Thomas' **STRENGTHS:**

After Lazarus death, he courageously told the other disciples they should go follow Jesus even in the midst of danger when Jesus' life was at risk.

👉 His **WEAKNESSES:**

Thomas deserted Jesus during the crucifixion. He demanded proof that Jesus had risen from the dead. His faith was based on seeing to believe. He had a tendency to see the worst in everything.

👉 His **REWARD & ACHIEVEMENTS:**

Thomas traveled with Jesus for three years. He was a missionary spreading the gospel to the east.

the TWELVE outlaws
T.S. Dobson

Why was Thomas **"WANTED!"** by Christ?

⇒ **His courage and his heroic pessimism.**

⇒ **His devotion to Christ.**

Background check: Thomas was known to have had a twin brother or sister, but this is not mentioned anywhere in the gospel. He's known as "Doubting Thomas" although scripture shows him in a more positive way. He was a man of slow belief. Before Christ he seemed pessimistic and saw things on the darker side. He was doubtful and worried about not seeing knowing his future.

Despite his worry and pessimism, Thomas loved Christ and was willing to die with Him rather than be without him. Jesus planned to go to Bethany which was a dangerous place to go because many had been killed for their beliefs there. Some of the disciples were afraid, but Thomas spoke up and said in John 11:16.

"Let us also go, that we may die with Him."

This was considered heroic pessimism at it's best. He knew Jesus was going into danger, but if this was what Christ needed to do then he was willing to go and die with Him. So even though we call this pessimistic it was an heroic gesture of his faith in Christ.

Thomas was written about in the Gospel of John. Most of Thomas' accomplishments for Christ came after the Lord's crucifixion and resurrection. He was not present when Jesus first appeared to the other disciples. This is where Thomas got his nickname of "Doubting Thomas."

the TWELVE outlaws
T.S. Dobson

When Jesus died, Thomas felt alone, abandoned, and somewhat forsaken. To deal with these emotions, Thomas purposefully separated himself from the group. When Jesus appeared in the Upper Room, after the resurrection. The other disciples were there and witnessed Jesus. Later the other disciples came to Thomas and told him they had seen the Lord, Thomas couldn't believe it. His doubting character was revealed when he said in John 20:25,

> Unless I see the nail marks in his hands and put my finger where the nails were, and put my hand into his side, I will not believe."

A week passed and Thomas was still feeling depressed about Jesus departure. Suddenly Jesus appeared to him and the other disciples who were staying in the house. Jesus said in John 20:26-29,

> "Peace be with you! Then he said to Thomas, "Put your finger here, see my hands. Reach out your hand and put it into my side. Stop doubting and believe." Thomas said to him, "My Lord and my God!" Then Jesus told him, "Because you have seen me, you have believed; blessed are those who have not seen and yet have believed."

Jesus was compassionate towards Thomas, even though Thomas had doubts. Jesus didn't scold Thomas for doubting. He actually invited Thomas to touch his wounds so he would believe.

Thomas' character even though he doubted, showed he had profound a love for Christ. Thomas' faith was restored.

All the disciples had doubts at times, but it was Thomas who put his doubts into words. Christ, in his time, came to comfort Thomas and show him he had risen from the dead and that he is Lord!

the TWELVE outlaws
T.S. Dobson

How can you relate and what can we learn from Thomas' life?

"I'll believe it when I see it!" We've all heard that line before and may have even said it ourselves a time or two. But believe it or not, that was how Thomas saw things. He was a skeptic in need of proof! He wanted evidence and demanding it quite often.

How many times have we related to Thomas' personality?

In today's society many hardheaded people want to witness such miracles or physically see Jesus before they will believe that he really exists. Even in Biblical times God ask the people to come by faith, not by sight! There were times that Jesus appeared to eyewitnesses before and after the crucifixion and resurrection. This was to strengthen their faith. It's no different today. We see miracles still today, by seeing God work in peoples lives through the Holy Spirit. Remember what Jesus said in John 20:29, he said that those who believe in Christ as Savior without seeing him (that's us) are blessed. God in heaven sympathizes with our uncertainty and negativity.

When Jesus comes into our hearts, he enables us to be able to see him working through us. Because of this we can trust him to one day deliver us from the pains and doubts of this world.

> History Fact: Traditions carry him east towards Persia or India where he was martyred. Thomas is commemorated by the Latin Church on December 21, the Greek Church on October 6, and by the Indians on July 1.

the TWELVE outlaws
T.S. Dobson

Concordance Study Time:

Using a Bible with a concordance in the back, find 5 verses about THOMAS. Write them down below. Write the Book and verse number only. This will be a quick reference for you on the apostle Thomas. Then go to those verses in the Bible and study them.

_____
_____
_____
_____
_____

Read the verses you jotted down above, then come up with your own version of what those verses mean to you. Study at least one of the verses you chose about the apostle Thomas. If you don't understand a term in the verse, look it up in the dictionary so that you can relate to what the Bible is saying to you.

_____
_____
_____
_____
_____
_____

(This page may be reproduced to use in a bible study group.)

the TWELVE outlaws
T.S. Dobson

Question & Answer Response:

1. What did you learn about apostle Thomas?

_____
_____
_____
_____

2. Name a strength and a weakness of Thomas?

_____
_____
_____
_____

3. Can you name an experience in your life where you can relate to Thomas?

_____
_____
_____
_____

Prayer Time:

Lord, thank you for teaching me about the Apostle Thomas. Help me to be like Thomas and turn my doubt and fear into faith and trust. Help me to show my love and trust is in you in all that I do. I ask these things in Jesus name. Amen.

(This page may be reproduced to use in a bible study group.)

John 3:16
For God so loved the world that he gave his one and only Son, that whoever believes in him shall not perish but have eternal life.

the NINTH outlaw

JAMES the Lesser or Little

Meaning of his name: "Supplanter", "the little", "the lesser", "the younger"

Apostle Profile

Father: Alphaeus

Mother: Mary (Mark 15:40), sister of the mother of Jesus, Mary

Brother(s): James the brother of our Lord, and other possible unknowns

Occupation: Apostle

Birth: Unknown

Death: Martyred by crucifixion in Egypt

James' (the little) **STRENGTHS:**

Jesus chose him to be a disciple. He was an unsung hero of faith.

His **WEAKNESSES:**

He deserted the Lord during his trial and crucifixion.

His **REWARD & ACHIEVEMENTS:**

It was possible James the little was the first to witness the risen Christ.

the TWELVE outlaws
T.S. Dobson

Why was James (the little) **"WANTED!"** by Christ?

⇒ **He was a quiet leader of the church.**

⇒ **Humble worker.**

Background check: Not much is written about the life of James "the less or little." What we do know is that there were several men names James in the Scriptures—James, son of Zebedee; James, son of Mary and Joseph (Jesus' half brother); James who wrote the Gospel that bears his name; and others. But this James was the son of Alphaeus. He is referred to as "James the less, or James the little" in Mark 15:40.

Why was he called less or little? It could have been a combination of things like — small in stature, young, and even a quiet natured person.

Like Andrew, James didn't have a bold nature. But he gave up everything to follow Christ. It took courage, faith, and love to follow Christ. This was heroic no matter how unseen or unheralded James the little appeared to be. He was still a follower and contributed to the spread of the Gospel of Christ.

James was the one who many consider was the first to see Christ after the resurrection.

1 Corinthians 15:7
Then he appeared to James, then to all the apostles.

Then the others disciples saw him, with the exception of Thomas, as we read about in the previous chapter.

the TWELVE outlaws
T.S. Dobson

> How can you relate and what can we learn from James' life?

Through the life of James the little, we see that every little deed we do for Christ, no matter how small, is just as important as the big deeds. Going out in the community and living by the Love of Christ gives witness to our character. You might feel insignificant or you don't think Christ can use you; but James the little was an ordinary man who did extraordinary things for God. He set an example for us. We can see how God uses men and women of all types.

Little James might have been small in stature and an unsung hero, but God still gave him power, glory and honor. God gave all these things to His disciples. And we are part of that same glory and honor. We are the body of Christ —today.

Psalm 115:1
Not to us, O Lord, not to us, but to your name give glory...

He didn't seek recognition or fame. God knows our hearts and wants us to have the same motivation.

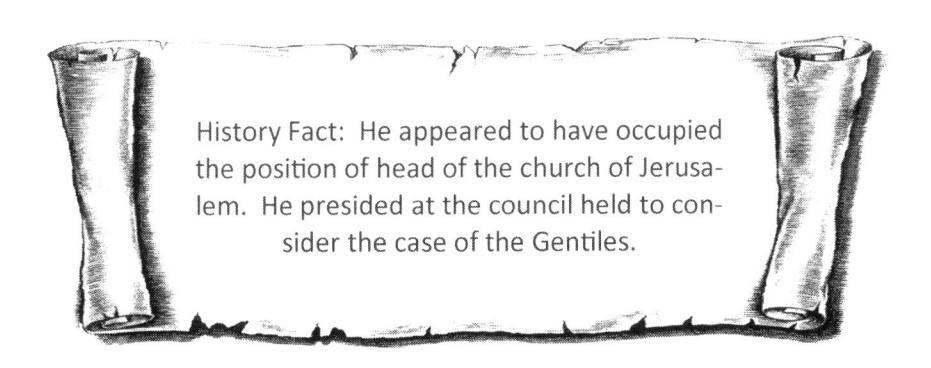

> History Fact: He appeared to have occupied the position of head of the church of Jerusalem. He presided at the council held to consider the case of the Gentiles.

the TWELVE outlaws
T.S. Dobson

Concordance Study Time:

Using a Bible with a concordance in the back, find 5 verses about JAMES the little. Write them down below. Write the Book and verse number only. This will be a quick reference for you on the apostle James. Then go to those verses in the Bible and study them.

_____
_____
_____
_____
_____

Read the verses you jotted down above, then come up with your own version of what those verses mean to you. Study at least one of the verses you chose about the apostle James. If you don't understand a term in the verse, look it up in the dictionary so that you can relate to what the Bible is saying to you.

_____
_____
_____
_____
_____
_____

(This page may be reproduced to use in a bible study group.)

the TWELVE outlaws
T.S. Dobson

Question & Answer Response:

1. What did you learn about apostle James the little?

_____
_____
_____
_____

2. Name a strength and a weakness of James the little?

_____
_____
_____
_____

3. Can you name an experience in your life where you can relate to James the little?

_____
_____
_____
_____

Prayer Time:

Lord, thank you for teaching me about the Apostle James the little. Help me to be like James and go out and be a beacon of light for you. I ask these things in Jesus name. Amen.

(This page may be reproduced to use in a bible study group.)

the TENTH outlaw

SIMON the Zealot—also known as Simon the Canaanite

Meaning of his name: "Zealot", "Peacemaker"

Apostle Profile

Death: He spread the gospel to Egypt as a missionary and was martyred in Persia.

the TWELVE outlaws
T.S. Dobson

☛ Simon's (the zealot) **STRENGTHS:**

Simon lived true to God's word after Jesus' ascension. He left everything he had to follow Christ.

☛ His **WEAKNESSES:**

Simon the Zealot deserted Jesus during his trial and crucifixion.

☛ His **REWARD & ACHIEVEMENTS:**

He was with the other disciples in the Upper Room in Jerusalem when Christ appeared to them.

☛ Why was Simon the Zealot **"WANTED!"** by Christ?

⇒ A counterbalance to Matthew the tax collector.

⇒ He was a Zealot.

Background check: Not much has been recorded about Simon the Zealot, other than his important call to be a disciple of Jesus Christ. There was some controversy about his role before coming to Christ, whether a Canaanite or a Zealot. The Zealots where considered a type of political party; a feared outlaw political sect. His occupation before becoming an apostle is unknown.

the TWELVE outlaws
T.S. Dobson

Simon the Zealot was a total opposite to the tax collecting Matthew. Zealots hated tax collectors and Romans. Maybe this is why Jesus chose Simon, to give a balance in political views. Even in the midst of having two totally different backgrounds, both Simon and Matthew came together as brothers in Christ; leaving behind their radical differences to spread the gospel of Jesus.

It seems that Simon the Zealot and Judas Iscariot were probably a team; but their differences were vast. Simon actually accepted Christ and became a loyal disciple and believer, whereas Judas never did.

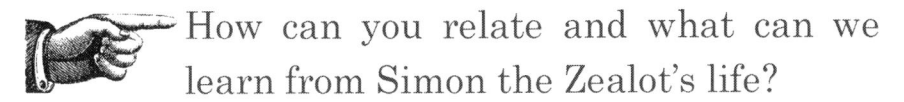

☞ How can you relate and what can we learn from Simon the Zealot's life?

Like Simon the Zealot, we might have different views with others at church or even in our daily journey. But we can be certain of one thing, if we are to be like Christ, we must come together as one body in Christ. We must spread the Good News to others. Because we have different opinions, its hard to get along with the ones that are most different from us. Only Christ can bridge differences, transcend political views, governments, and all earthly suffering you may face. Following Jesus leads to reconciliation, salvation, and heaven.

the **TWELVE** outlaws
T.S. Dobson

Concordance Study Time:

Using a Bible with a concordance in the back, find 5 verses about SIMON the Zealot. Write them down below. Write the Book and verse number only. This will be a quick reference for you on the apostle Simon. Then go to those verses in the Bible and study them.

_____
_____
_____
_____
_____

Read the verses you jotted down above, then come up with your own version of what those verses mean to you. Study at least one of the verses you chose about the apostle Simon. If you don't understand a term in the verse, look it up in the dictionary so that you can relate to what the Bible is saying to you.

_____
_____
_____
_____
_____
_____

(This page may be reproduced to use in a bible study group.)

the TWELVE outlaws
T.S. Dobson

Question & Answer Response:

1. What did you learn about apostle Simon the Zealot?

_____
_____
_____
_____

2. Name a strength and a weakness of Simon?

_____
_____
_____
_____

3. Can you name an experience in your life where you can relate to Simon?

_____
_____
_____
_____

Prayer Time:

Lord, thank you for teaching me about the Apostle Simon the Zealot. Help me to be like Simon and overcome my differences with those I come in contact with so that I may give testimony and witness for Christ. I ask these things in Jesus name. Amen.

(This page may be reproduced to use in a bible study group.)

Jude 20-21
But you, dear friends, build yourselves up in your most holy faith and pray in the Holy Spirit. Keep yourselves in God's love as you wait for the mercy of our Lord Jesus Christ to bring you to eternal life.

the ELEVENTH outlaw

THADDAEUS—also known as Judas or Jude

Meaning of his name: "giver of joy", "praise", Thaddaeus means "courageous or great-hearted one"

Apostle Profile

Father: Clopas

Mother: Mary, cousin of the mother of Jesus Mary

Brother: James the Zealot

Occupation: Apostle

Death: Found the church Edessa where he was martyred.

the TWELVE outlaws
T.S. Dobson

👉 Thaddaeus STRENGTHS:

Through all the hardships and persecutions. Thaddaeus was loyal and continued to serve Christ. He learned about the gospel directly from Jesus.

👉 His WEAKNESSES:

Thaddaeus abandoned Jesus during his trial and crucifixion.

👉 Thaddaeus REWARD & ACHIEVEMENTS:

Thaddaeus was a missionary. He penned the book of Jude. The Book of Jude expresses praise to God; one of the finest in the New Testament.

👉 Why was Thaddaeus "WANTED!" by Christ?

⇒ **Loyalty**

⇒ **Tender-hearted**

Background check: Little is known about Thaddaeus. From what we know, he was chosen by Christ to be a disciple. His first name was Judas, but as to not get confused with Judas Iscariot (the betrayer) Thaddaeus' full name was Judas Lebbaeus Thaddaeus. We will discuss Judas Iscariot in the final chapter. He was given the name Thaddaeus because of his sweet childlike nature.

Biblical accounts of Thaddaeus took place in the Upper Room. In John 14:21,

> Jesus said, "He who has My commandments and keeps them, it is he who loves Me. And who loves Me will be loved by My Father, and I will love him and manifest Myself to him." Judas Thaddaeus asked, "Lord, how is it that You will manifest Yourself to us, and not to the world?" Jesus tenderly answers, "If anyone loves Me, he will keep My word; and Will come to him and make Our home with him."

Because Thaddaeus sincerely asked this question in John 14:21, Christ, answered him generously. The way he responded was just as powerful and reaching as the other well known disciples.

Thaddaeus was known as preaching the gospel of Jesus Christ after his resurrection through missionary work.

Thaddaeus warns in the book of Jude to avoid false teachers who twist the gospel for their own purposes. He also emphasized that we must defend the Christian faith daily.

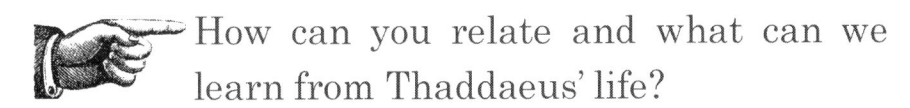

How can you relate and what can we learn from Thaddaeus' life?

You may not be an outspoken person, or perhaps you're shy and keep to yourself. You wonder how you can make a difference? God says you don't have to wonder! Just by living according to the Bible and reading it shows your love for Christ. It also shows that you believe Christ died on the cross for your sins. By living for God and praying to Him, the Holy Spirit will guide your steps! Being sincere and genuine toward others is a way to show God's love.

the TWELVE outlaws
T.S. Dobson

Concordance Study Time:

Using a Bible with a concordance in the back, find 5 verses about THADDAEUS. Write them down below. Write the Book and verse number only. This will be a quick reference for you on the apostle Thaddaeus. Then go to those verses in the Bible and study them.

_____
_____
_____
_____
_____

Read the verses you jotted down above, then come up with your own version of what those verses mean to you. Study at least one of the verses you chose about the apostle Thaddaeus. If you don't understand a term in the verse, look it up in the dictionary so that you can relate to what the Bible is saying to you.

_____
_____
_____
_____
_____
_____

(This page may be reproduced to use in a bible study group.)

the TWELVE outlaws
T.S. Dobson

Question & Answer Response:

1. What did you learn about apostle Thaddaeus?

_____
_____
_____
_____

2. Name a strength and a weakness of Thaddaeus?

_____
_____
_____
_____

3. Can you name an experience in your life where you can relate to Thaddaeus?

_____
_____
_____
_____

Prayer Time:

Lord, thank you for teaching me about the Apostle Thaddaeus. Help me to be like Thaddaeus and be sincere and tender-hearted when needed towards others. I ask these things in Jesus name. Amen.

(This page may be reproduced to use in a bible study group.)

Mark 14:43
Just as he was speaking, Judas, one of the Twelve, appeared. With him was a crowd armed with swords and clubs, sent from the chief priests, the teachers of the law, and the elders.

the TWELFTH outlaw

JUDAS Iscariot

Meaning of his name: "Praise", "Dagger-man"

Apostle Profile

Father: Simon

Occupation: Apostle

Birth: Judean City of Kerioth

Death: Near Jerusalem

the TWELVE outlaws
T.S. Dobson

👉 Judas Iscariot **STRENGTHS:**

Even though Judas betrayed Jesus he did feel remorse after the fact.

Matthew 27:3-5
When Judas, who had betrayed him, saw that Jesus was condemned, he was seized with remorse and returned the thirty silver coins to the chief priests and the elders...So Judas threw the money into the temple and left. Then he went away and hanged himself.

👉 His **WEAKNESSES:**

Judas was a thief. He sometimes stole from the money bag that the group put him in charge of.

👉 His **REWARD & ACHIEVEMENTS:**

One of Jesus' original disciples. He traveled with Jesus studying under him for three years. He went with the other disciples; sent out by Jesus to cast-out demons.

the TWELVE outlaws
T.S. Dobson

Why was Judas Iscariot "WANTED!" by Christ?

⇒ **Money handler.**

Background check: Judas is the son of Simon. His surname is Iscariot which means a man of Kerioth. He came from far away to join the group, none of the other disciples knew of him. Unlike the other disciples, he had a guarded heart, which he never gave to Jesus. Instead his heart belonged to the political and material world. The other disciples were caught off guard; never suspecting his schemes. It didn't take long before Judas became disillusioned. He was in charge for the money of the group and would steal from the bag in the dark. He eventually turned his greed into hate for others and Christ. Jesus had been kind to Judas, but he started to experience an evil nature. Gradually, after "Satan entered into him," he betrayed Jesus.

John 13:26-27
Jesus answered, "It is the one to who I will give this piece of bread when I have dipped it in the dish." Then, dipping the piece of bread, he gave it to Judas Iscariot, son of Simon. As soon as Judas took the bread, Satan entered into him.

Once this happened, he followed through and betrayed Jesus. He felt extreme guilt for the betrayal. He couldn't handle what he had done.

Judas Iscariot made the biggest mistake in history.

Matthew 26:13-15
Then one of the Twelve-the one called Judas Iscariot-went to the chief priests and asked, "What are you willing to give me if I hand him over to you?" So they counted out for him thirty silver coins.

Judas was genuinely sorry for what he had done to Jesus, and had no intention on turning him in to be killed. He just wanted more money, and thought Jesus would be punished, but not killed. Of course the chief priests and elders had no intention of letting Jesus go. Their intentions were to place him on a trial and crucify him. When they came for Jesus, Judas felt sorrow and remorse for what he had done and threw down the money in shame. He realized he couldn't take it back.

Instead of accepting what he had done to Jesus was wrong and ask forgiveness, he ran away from Jesus. Judas failed to seek Christ's forgiveness. He was thinking it was too late and he ended his life in suicide.

Matthew 27:3-5
When Judas, who had betrayed him, saw that Jesus was condemned, he was seized with remorse and returned the thirty silver coins to the chief priests and the elders...So Judas threw the money into the temple and left. Then he went away and hanged himself.

Why Judas was chosen to be a disciple of Christ is not known to some. But what we do know, is that Jesus knew from the beginning that Judas would betray him. It was a part of God's plan. Judas' motives for betraying Jesus was led by evil greed.

Sadly, he never cried out to God. He never asked for mercy. He silenced the voice of guilt with suicide. Judas betrayed Christ and in effect sold his soul to the devil.

Luke: 22:47-48
He (Judas) approached Jesus to kiss him, but Jesus asked him, "Judas, are you betraying the Son of Man with a kiss?"

How can you relate and what can we learn from Judas Iscariot's life?

God taught us an important life lesson in the betrayal Judas performed. We can show an outward appearance of righteousness when we go to church and do the right things, but we can still be a lost person. If we don't understand and accept what Jesus has done for us, going to church will be just for show. It doesn't mean much to be good and go to church if you don't truly believe in your heart that Jesus has saved you from a sinful world. You must live by the Holy Spirit. If we are to lean on Him and not our own understanding, we have to give up the selfish control of our life.

There may be times in your life where you feel hopeless and feel like God won't forgive you for what you have said or done. This is a lie from the devil. God is forgiving and just. No matter how large the sin is that you have committed, no sin is too big for God to forgive.

You must deal with sin, ask forgiveness, and watch God transform your life. Turn away from the sin that is causing you to stumble. I can't tell you the countless times I have gone to God with sincere prayer about sin and situations in my life. He was faithful and just to forgive me from it.

Sadly, Judas missed a very important opportunity to walk closely by Jesus' side. He missed the most important message in Christ's ministry. Even though he betrayed Christ, he could have asked for forgiveness and received it.

It's possible to be near Christ and still be totally hardened by sin. No matter how evil the attempt may be, it cannot stop God's will and purpose.

the TWELVE outlaws
T.S. Dobson

Concordance Study Time:

Using a Bible with a concordance in the back, find 5 verses about JUDAS Iscariot. Write them down below. Write the Book and verse number only. This will be a quick reference for you on the apostle Judas Iscariot. Then go to those verses in the Bible and study them.

_____
_____
_____
_____
_____

Read the verses you jotted down above, then come up with your own version of what those verses mean to you. Study at least one of the verses you chose about the apostle Judas Iscariot. If you don't understand a term in the verse, look it up in the dictionary so that you can relate to what the Bible is saying to you.

_____
_____
_____
_____
_____
_____

(This page may be reproduced to use in a bible study group.)

the TWELVE outlaws
T.S. Dobson

Question & Answer Response:

1. What did you learn about apostle Judas Iscariot?

2. Name a strength and a weakness of Judas Iscariot?

3. Can you name an experience in your life where you can relate to Judas Iscariot?

Prayer Time:

Lord, thank you for teaching me about the Apostle Judas Iscariot. Help me to realize my sins and ask for forgiveness from them. Help me to be more committed to Christ. To lean on the Holy Spirit for comfort and protection. I ask these things in Jesus name. Amen.

(This page may be reproduced to use in a bible study group.)

Plan of Salvation

Are we true believers of Christ or secret pretenders? If we fail, do we give up hope? Do we accept his forgiveness and seek His truth?

With all the disciples faults and character flaws, they were ordinary men carrying out the ministry of Jesus before and after the ascension. Their ministry continues as we read about their lives in the Bible. God empowered these men to be his disciples and now it's our turn to make a difference and spread the gospel. People like you and me are the instruments to send the message of God's love to the ends of the earth. First we must know that we are saved.

John 3:16
"For God loved the world so much, that He gave his one and only son so that everyone that believes in him will not perish, but have Eternal life."

How can I be saved? The steps to salvation are as easy as
A.B.C.

ADMIT—Admit that you are a sinner in need of God.

BELIEVE—That Jesus died and rose again for your sins.

CONFESS—That Jesus Christ is Lord of your life.

Romans 10:13
"Whoever calls on the name of the Lord shall be saved."

Your salvation experience is the beginning of your personal relationship with Jesus Christ.

You must now say the sinners prayer:

Lord Jesus,

I know I am sinner and need your forgiveness. I know you died on the cross for me. I now turn from my sins and ask you to forgive me. I now invite you into my heart and life. I now trust you as Savior and follow you as Lord. Thank you for saving me. Amen.

Scripture promises if you have accepted Christ:

1 John 5:11-13
And the witness is this, that God has given us eternal life, and this life is in His Son. 12He who has the Son has the life; he who does not have the Son of God does not have the life. 13These things I have written to you who believe in the name of the Son of God, in order that you may know that you have eternal life.

If you have prayed the above prayer or one like it for the first time please let us know so we can rejoice with you and pray for you. Email: teresadobson1@aol.com. If you have a church family let them know of your decision. If you don't have a church, find one close to you so you can worship the Lord and fellowship with other believers.

the TWELVE outlaws
T.S. Dobson

How can you make changes in your life like the disciples?

Peter: Spokesman—if you are a good spokesman like Peter and someone who is a leader; God can use you to spread his word and tell others about Jesus. Don't speak to soon and watch what you say. Let God help you make the right decisions and say the right things.

Andrew: If you aren't a spokesman you can still reach out to others by finding ways to reach one person at a time.

James son of Zebedee: Show that you have passion for Christ and that you're willing to walk with him in a real relationship. Study the Bible to arm yourself with the Word.

John: Show the Fruit of the Holy Spirit called love toward others; even when they may not deserve it.

Philip: Don't see the negative in a situation, but always look for the good and live by faith in the Lord.

Bartholomew: Always know that God is watching over you, and wants a strong relationship with you every day.

Thomas: When you feel alone, trust God for protection in every situation. Don't depend on your own understanding!

Matthew: Don't put your trust in material things and earthly power. Lean on the power of God and trust Him for your needs.

James the Lesser or littler: You can find ways in the small or little things you do for Christ to make a difference.

Thaddaeus: Learn to be tender and open minded to help others.

Simon the Zealot: Learn to live by the laws of God, and not worldly politics.

Judas Iscariot: Use the Fruit of the Holy Spirit called Self-control in your Christian walk; don't be fake and always repent of the sin in your life.

So what do I do now?

Be an **OUTLAW** for God! Stand up for Christ and what he did for you! Read your Bible, pray, and seek the truth!

Jesus paid the price for us to get out of earthly bondage. Look to the law of God for answers in the Bible. This will help you correct your **OUTLAW** tendencies. There will always be good and evil on earth. The reward is great! Jesus paid our bail bonds, and we are free. Living by the law of God we will gain an Eternal reward. Living without God means we are heavily chained to an Eternal punishment with Satan.

BREAK THE CHAINS!

As you look to become a disciple for Christ, read the Bible for guidance to know where you are being led in the Holy Spirit.

You are **"WANTED"** by **CHRIST!**

NOTES

NOTES

NOTES

NOTES

Made in the USA
Monee, IL
28 November 2019